Upon Arrival

Poems by
Paula Cisewski

Black Ocean
Boston · New York · Chicago

To reprint, reproduce, or transmit electronically, or by recording all or part of *Upon Arrival*, beyond brief excerpts for reviews or educational purposes, please send a written request to the publisher at:

BLACK OCEAN
P.O. Box 990962
Boston, MA 02199
www.blackocean.org

Cover Design by Star St. Germain
www.thisisstar.com

ISBN 978-0-9777709-2-2

Library of Congress Cataloging-in-Publication Data

Cisewski, Paula, 1968-
Upon arrival : poems / by Paula Cisewski.
p. cm.
I. Title.

PS3603.I84U66 2006
811'.6--dc22
2006001145

Printed and bound in the United States of America.

FIRST EDITION

For Anton.

Contents

Upon Arrival

Grateful acknowledgement is made to the editors of the following magazines and presses who originally published the following poems, or versions of them:

Conduit: "The Word String Can't Blister Your Hands"

Fuori:One: "Below Freezing," "Gimme Shelter," "Gold Rush Hamlet," "Origami"

Swerve: "Peace"

Spout: "Lucky Poem"

Fuori:Two: "Opening Remarks," "Our Possible Brother," "Springtime," "Passenger Villanelle"

Puppy Flowers: "Springtime," "Here On Somnambulist Avenue," "Ear Ache Song," "According To Cloud Formations I will Spend This Day"

Spinning Jenny: "How Birds Work"

Melic Review: "Piano Solo"

SHADE: "Daedalian," "To A Margin," "Birds of Appetite," "My Dearest   Memory"

Black Warrior Review: "Mercury Waits Tables At The Macrocosm Cafe"

Forklift, Ohio: "The Motto For Anyone Who Falls Into A Black Hole Must Be 'Think Imaginary'"

Crazyhorse: "Common Prayer"

Hunger Mountain: "History, A Round"

Some of the poems in this book were originally published as a limited edition, fine press chapbook titled *How Birds Work* by Fuori Editions.

I would also like to express gratitude to Kenny Horst, Sarah Fox, Davis Wilson, Stephanie Bessire, Gabriella Klein, Ralph Angel, Mary Ruefle, Jack Myers, Roger Weingarten, 77% Breakfast, my family, the legendary punk rock drummer Anton Winter, Peter Schimke, and the Lewis clan. And to Sarah Jacobson.

ALL THE WAY HOME

The apron pocket in me.
The broken car horn in me.
The greenfinch in me flying straight into
the cracked mirror in me.
And the front porch light in me
calling to the midnight in me.
The harvest: the amaranth, the wheat.
The natural bridge in me.
The calculus. The birthday cake.
The Walt Whitman in me finds me scrumptious.
Including the smokestack and leftover dinosaur in me.
The emperor in me placed himself in charge
of the olive branch in me. The waitress in me
sneezes in his glass of hundred year old port.
The story I read in me.
The *you-already-said-that* in me.
The firewalk: the glow, the blistered faith.
When the god in me is
good, it scrambles to pick up
the waitress's dropped napkins. And
when it is bad it is horrid. It's the left-
you-at-the-altar in me, crying me
mee meee all the way home.

Fallings From Us

It was with regret that we passed every turn
of this charming path, where every new picture
was purchased by the loss of another which we
would never have been tired of gazing at.

– **William Wordsworth**

TYROS' WORLD TOUR

Each of us captaining
a solitary lifeboat.
As if we are lost
at sea. We've never
been to sea. We studied
the Triumphant Explorers of Celluloid
and acted as if we ourselves weathered
their expeditions, could now
shed arctic layers. We
shivered at the thought. As if none
of us will ever be a dead body in our lives.
Which we logically won't.
Therefore, our further lives are
to be one astounding caper:
our mothers' cheeks streaked
with sudden maternal pride!
Because each lifeboat appeared
like a Polaroid of a heart,
we are pulling our boats
together with rope. And then
we will name the rope.

BELOW FREEZING

In our homes, the lonely fairy
godmother of moths and dust smokes cigarettes,
leans a whiskered cheek on the drapery
as she fingers the frosted sash, gazing out.

The sky has spent days mimicking
the color of a liar's best business suit.
It's getting in our lungs, through
the wool of our children's caps.

We recognize our neighbors only
by their shovels and salt. Nothing
moves us as we carve out our days. But
somewhere, there is a party every night.

A champagne bottle pops
inside a glowing room as we take tiny, careful
steps in our best heels up a treacherous walk.
Hold out your arms.

THE MOTTO FOR ANYONE WHO FALLS INTO A BLACK HOLE MUST BE "THINK IMAGINARY."

Stephen Hawking said that. A motto
for when everything's a long way off
like the stars we won't be able to see tonight
or eternity consisting entirely of nows
is how I think Dickinson said it. Chugga chugga,
another Wednesday, is how I say it.
Seems like words are more
compressed than they used to be. Like snow—
a large task broken down by the sky—
all the nows falling gently around us.
The days have so many heartbeats inside
chugga chugga motoring them along,
or as in *One Hundred Years of Solitude*,
the whole town of Macondo living the same day
over and over again. It has been Winter here
for so long and there are limits to how far
I can retreat into my home or my Wednesday,
the quiet little nows melting on my cheek.
I, quote, make nothing happen: I survive
in the valley of my saying, unquote. Plus I read
a lot. Which reminds me once in the long DMV line
I had a paperback version of *Crime and Punishment*
in my coat pocket and this guy behind me noticed
and actually described a passage where Svidrigailov
describes Raskolnikov's solitary garret
as a coffin and I wanted to say Yes I *loved*
that! But I couldn't; I wasn't to that part.
I don't remember, later, ever getting to that part!
Did we read different books with the same
characters? I felt then as if
for my whole life I'd know nothing

but Wednesday. It seems like if we're going
to have this much more night we should
do something more beautiful with it than
drive to yet another party where the talk
will drink its way from feta to fate: who
authored us so predictably?? Are these all
the same heartbeats repeating?
It can't be: the snow is piled up higher than ever.
Two things I do understand about science are gravity
and evaporation. Think about moisture rising and what
it's absorbed: trainwhistle, breath of someone reading
aloud alone, a jingle from the postman's transistor radio.
Think how, without the soft falling of these things,
we'd never see the stars again.

EAR ACHE SONG

The garbler sifts the garble
from the spice. The word

drops through language after language
and is garbled. No spice.
                            I learned
just recently that I have always
misused the word recant
and it has nothing to do with singing.
                            Not again.

Here is a proper sentence:
My husband says my hair is "grandiose"
then RECANTS the GARBLED compliment.

                    When I was small I thought
this particular ache was called
an "ear rag" because when I had one,
my mother would hold a warm towel to my head.
Something finally would
                    pop
and then everyone suddenly
would cease their singing.

GIMME SHELTER

Keith Richards was waiting again last night–kicked back in
a velvet lounge of stuffed chairs, smoking

when I entered the dream, biting my nails. "Sugar," he
rasped, "relaaaax..." and smiled, every crevice of his face
folding in like the split feathers of wings. I stopped biting
my nails and sat back. We had a "highball." I clacked my
ice around

in my glass as though it was my first "highball" and now I
get to say "highball." Leisurely, time passed. He spoke
low to me about the wankers I should shrug off, the car
insurance past due, then a few new anecdotes on The Rock
and Roll Life. I nod. I know. *Yeaaah. I know.*

"It's funny," I felt myself blurting, "I don't even listen to
your music..." Immediate regret. But he couldn't have
cared less. "Tssk tssk," he teased, the big skull ring on his
middle finger wagging back and forth, back and forth, like
a watch on a chain, or maybe it was more like rocking. A
very small crib.

THE PLAYTHING

The crawling baby discovers
a shadow on the wall.
He crawls up to it. He slaps
the shadow hand.
He slaps the shadow head. It looks
like a baby; the baby doesn't get it!
Slats of light from the picture window
frame the baby and his new plaything.
He keeps toying with the shadow.
Good baby! This is as good as a birthday.
He wants to crawl right into the wall
where the shadow is. Kill it
kill it the mommy giggles because
the baby thinks its shadow is a game.
The grandparents pick up cameras
and photograph the moment,
which doesn't stay as
precious. But anyway the baby has
already forgotten its shadow, distracted
by the bright toys on the floor. When
he tumbles the yellow blocks,
he doesn't notice the little shadow
hand underneath his own, also playing.

TO A MARGIN

– for/after Sarah Fox

Dear S,
The shape of time is not stone
today, it is forward.
Not less than arrows
or the speed of height.
No more stone than
what equals sand
-(-x) thousands.
Today the shape of time
is softer than death plus one.
Stop-winged but infinitely sky.
Adding positives to negatives
at a chalkboard until
you want to pass out
in front of the upper classmen.

Dear S,
The shape of time leaves
shadows we call "I made this"
we call "memories" we call
"smoking." There shift scenes,
a bad actor's shadow over
all the lines greased down
a squeaky face who reads
"but I feel nineteeeeen."
Kill mirrors.

Dear S,
Today the shape of time
is mimicking your shape thinking
Babies? I could have babies...

Dear S,
Solution is the way
our play bodies take everything in,
make anything, including terrible stops
and detailed paintings of lives. Still. We dissolve.
Time and salt have the whitest wedding.
I think I'll cry real tears
every second it happens.

Dear S,
Yes.
Time with its stone shape
did then *renounce it all to a margin*.

Dear S,
The push of a tree
throwing leaves at you: Fall-time.
I know orange like a stone's seed.
Like an orange.
Time lurks / time couldn't
care less about lurking.
It's so omnipresent
it forgets itself before we do.
Tying our shoes for work
we did bore / are boring
will bore time to death.

Dear S,
You know every little pebble
in a highway (la la la?) Time
could only want knees
to skin on each.

MY DEAREST   MEMORY

> In this dream I must selectively
> apply the law of gravity to myself
> or I fly off the world.

My father is taking place
on a boat watching the sunset.
He wears his reading glasses

> Not a dream, a memory: this is

the real day I am flying
off the dock because
One Must Learn To Swim   Sometime.
                      As I am falling,
my father occurs to me
as the best audience
the sky has ever had:

> He never interrupts.

Wait. Did my father wear glasses?
It must not be him in the boat.

                    Plunged cold
Memory of   water in my lungs
a memory   the whole sky is lost
I do remember   someone always saves me
remembering it   hilarious to breathe
vividly   once saved

                        Oh yes,
my father happens
to have always worn glasses.
It is him. Or else he is
wearing his glasses someplace else.
                        Another real time.
If that is him
out in the middle of the lake,
who pushes me in? And who
eventually fishes me out?

LITERARY WORK

And if you find yourself
in the midst of a stifling jungle

you can look way up
toward the canopy and focus

on a single branch.
That branch is a literary device. It creaks

in a distant breeze. But
a thousand white feathers falling

from a brick cloud form silence,
which is another literary device.

The sound of a broken doorbell
instills the important literary device

called desire. Memory is a lost scarf;
guess what that is. And dust

is also a literary device. Floating
in the office sunbeams. Dust is

mostly comprised of human skin as we
slake away from ourselves.

After a period of disuse, the keys
of my typewriter covered with

a thin layer of literary devices.

OUR POSSIBLE BROTHER

This is a magic, it does

not have to be a body attached to
a lovely noun such as "a brother."

Take ours for example. You can say him
but can you prove him? We believe

he has populated a small Mexican village; it's him
children the world around all call

by different names. He made your license plate and
still you can't prove him. Why

would you want to prove him? He is
our brother. Here

he is in the plinks of a pebble
skipping the big lake. He is a great

skipper. But now

our pebble's gone for good.
Our pebble. Not our brother.

OTHER WAYS TO SAY NO

~ Little Napoleon.

~ Memory with its tweezers and monocle
 neatly gluing the *yes* into *yes*-terday.

~ Blueprint for a fortress replete with
 markings of where it will crumble.

~ Yes is
 sometimes used alone in
 inquiry, as no is used,
 especially by the French, *non?*
 In that case yes and no are synonyms.

~ Reduction.

~ When life gets ya down enough to wish everything
 could stay still as a moment in a master drawing, yes
 is the drawing's giant eraser. Each fleck
 of eraser dust is one way to say no.

~ Camouflage.

~ Once I said "now" and the person
 I was speaking to thought I said "no."
 It was very important that I explained.

~ Triumph.

~ Pity the poor little No
                that needs so much!

                        Who cannot bear to be alone!

        We function as its attachments
    .   so it can have something
                            to do "un" to.

~ A big No-No can and must succeed
                because we love it
                            and feel sorry for it. Plus
        we like how it feels naughty like a biker jacket.
                Poor vacuum I'll feed you.
                            Poor petite No without clothes.
        Poor poor machine gun we
            silence. We silence:
                    nonononononononononononononono

~ Or, Simple No: just going back to sleep.

~ Brush the dust off the work table
    onto the wood floor. Do you like
    the color of this room we're in? It's called
    crawl-back-in-the-egg-shell blue. Or, answer true,
    would you rather be excused now?

TELESCOPE PSALM

Am I afraid to be forgiven?
I'd have to wear nicer suits.

By the time everything is fair I will
have devised a system to send word

via the birds on my roof. But I am
of two minds about most subjects

and, in turns, one mind must elbow the other
who is snoring. That's why I thought I enjoyed

talking too much tonight at the brewpub
until the silence of the long walk home

made a better argument, better
company. The sky's library of stars and dust,

whatever is possible remaining possible
even as it's gazed at through the private

telescopes of an entire hemisphere.
It's now. It's not forever. And this

forever shall be true. To see further,
those without telescopes sometimes

cup their hands around their eyes.

ORIGAMI

1.

A helicopter looking for a good story
chops air under charcoal folds of cloud.
Sheets of sun squeak through the cracks.

We are gray people with buds on.
Desires like feeble wings unfurl.
We are river people.   The river

makes the news every night: the way
light shimmers down it like thousands of dimes,
something misunderstood as a promise of flight.

2.

A man's hat glides downstream like a prize paper boat.

3.

He makes her a ring from a one dollar bill.
She likes it, and makes him a silver crane

the size of a pinky fingernail
from the foil of her cigarette pack.

Then the bill for her coffee comes. She pays
and goes, though they may have spoken the same language.

Something folds out in the shape of a bloom
for the pocket of quiet they guard with their lives.

MOTHER'S DAY #14

...thirteen, baker's dozen, twenty, score; hundred,
century, centenary; thousand, million, billion, trillion;
zero (see INSUBSTANTIALITY.)
> – from Roget's Thesaurus
> under "numeration"

Big boy
    on a little
        boy's bike, nothing

is enlisted
    in this park
        but pigeons. Early

Spring has
    erupted brown, and we
        wade through

your difference.
    Your head,
        ahead,

has won a race
    to a line in the air.
        Above me, above news

and scraps
    on the wind;
        how did you

discover this
　　　　plan for increase? I wanted
　　　　　　us to remain

forever
　　　　no older: I'd be
　　　　　　a white first

communion dress
　　　　like a leaf
　　　　　　on a tree in a box

labeled "Last October."
　　　　But your protector.
　　　　　　As a container

for time I am imperfect,
　　　　easily obliterated.
　　　　　　This is a common flaw.

Yet fresh colors
　　　　and we
　　　　　　ensue.

One Mississippi...
　　　　Two Mississippi...
　　　　　　To sing hush-a-bye

was beautiful,
　　　　is beautiful, is
　　　　　　not now required.

GOLD RUSH HAMLET

I will come father by father
until a fatherless son is unoriginal.
I will not pity myself for the weight

of a woman's gowns. Night
is night. I will breathe.
But first, I want

pictographic records
of how every person lives
their life. A multiplication lesson
to equal the universal mind.

I want a trail of lessons, a railroad
to the West. A pipeline.
I want possession of the absolute

rule of freedom. I will
sit window still until
I'm sure, resisting the urge

to live in history. I have a sieve,
I'll shake time out.
I will know something.
Damn it! What does the indifferent

spider-eye of God divide
down into, but any part
of the world, and a man?

LOVE POEM

The clouds fall out of each other.

The weatherman fears for his good suit.

In the rain, my lover works, carving

rivulets into stone, rivulets into stone.

Someone's got to bring the sheets in off the line.

Leaves shudder as birds perch in them.

The perched birds shudder back.

 # How Birds Work

—It was passed from one bird to another,
the whole gift of the day.

– Pablo Neruda
from "Bird"

A SMALL ROCK

Like lost showgirls,
a laundry-white flock
of peacocks wanders

the grounds of Madison Zoo.
A caged crow is the star.
It is albino. Hard to believe—

a white crow! It could be
mistaken for a dove.
Someone throws a small rock

to make it caw.
I move on, hating the world:
I wanted to hear it too.

How deeply now I love
the snow leopard.
I name and name him:

Philosopher, Ascetic, Fool.
I want my head between his jaws
as he hunches, back to the bars

watching shadows
of birds on the wall.

DAEDALIAN

...your cobbled wings
then struck me: blue,
soon to be as absent as sky.
What could I have said midflight?
                   "The keel in your breast, boy!"   *?*
A blue cage in my mouth,
shameful sediment of desire.
How you spiraled and arced,
the smoking wax in my throat.
After the plunge of your body,
                  a single feather
        then another
    and another
papered the vast sea.
(Where was the crone that morning
with her uninvited forecast?
I'm tired of hearing about what we did do)

: your foolishness, my foolishness.

I am now prepared
to feel my way down the dark sides
of the riddles unto death.
O do be wordless.
Something sweet and red
fertilizes regret:
sugar rotting the apple.
The thrum of our hearts, or
Beat...   Beat...
The worked muscle of strong wingbones.
A series of fortunes. A long story
always eventually stopped short.
                And still, we flew

INSIDE THE MEMORY WORKS

Whatever has been lost
              deteriorated into a word
                             for itself
comes home in echoes.
                   Home. Comes home
to this clock tower where sparrows roost.
Their slight weights changing
the escapement's tock
                   tock
and thereby the entire mechanism
slightly. Sparrows grow older, coo,
and sleep huddled: plumb-bobs
              bereft of syntax, too.

Echoes do please and insulate goldenly:
a "heavenly" aura of absence from now.

HE MAY NOT BE DEAD; HE STILL HAS WINGS
– for Michael

The small selves we then were are

                    not here for questioning.
                    Somewhere

                    grown, he
            is not without me.
    I am surely stunted within him,

                    a girl forever

                winning or whining,

                    remembered

(Don't *within*   and *without*   sound   opposite?)

                of a brother.

A memory of brother:
    a cowboy bandana. A bb-
            gun-shoe-shooter   brother boy

        then BANG!   No grown man

                counts   backward from absence.

Nothing can mark him.   Look again.

            Not even a stone.
            (a head stone)

So how does a lost brother stay

(he stays)　　　　singing,　　　　voice of the failed

　　　thief within　　　　　　a grown woman?

　　　　　　By becoming

　a shell game,　　　the word

　　　　bottle,

　　　　a theory　　　　of flight–

a strange man who was
　　　　　　named
　　　　　　　twice with emerald wings:

　　　　the painter of the magician's dove for a girl
　　　　who has learned to sister his going.

SPRINGTIME

The sky never fills with any leftover flying.
– Li-Young Lee

A cardinal cat-calls
the morning. Bawdy-songed, he calls
the day like a cat: daring
a "cute" predator with sleep inside it.

A lonely bird, or he wouldn't sing
near us. Desiring out loud. At us?
Let's don't feel bad,
he is singing *with* us. What

is that winter bird doing singing
redly between the tight green buds?
Will Spring cancel him?
Will a cancelled bird leave room for

?
Like inside people,
how we have so many
birds not in our hearts?

THE DISAPPEARING WOMAN TRICK

Draw any conclusion you want: I love
your sleeve, not you. Or truly I love

what's up there: the entire suit of hearts, possibly,
about to appear in the hand tattooed *were what longed*.

    In which slights are bedded:
    The taste of elsewhere.
    Still you need an assistant.

                I expect

the queen I choose to be the card you guess.
However will you.   Keep me as your rube,

your shill,   I want   coins plucked

from my ear, each and every color of canary
to escape
        your hat
            and feather
                my heart.

              (What can

    not surrender does not
    surrender but does not
    necessarily keep well.)

            But I believe!

Every best thing passes through itself
like silver rings. Now ask me
to enter the box and pull the curtain.

As I unhinge the trap door, you will

announce to the crowd: One minute
you see her. The next, you don't!

ACCORDING TO CLOUD FORMATIONS
I WILL SPEND THIS DAY
– in memory of P.M.

lit by crows wherein thinking for a long minute I think
ideas in and out like clouds. As likened to a flight pattern.
That cloud looks like a crow. That cloud looks like an idea.
Yesterday I had to try harder to appreciate everything. I
wondered where the time goes. Tucked in a date book.
Every day gone when it can't be stopped. My going hands
distract; they are papery crows. They would turn every
corner into a neat month of edible days. As likened to a
flight pattern. Clouds pad the sky, are slow. Regally, they
can take any shape, such as of something alive. Real crows
swoop, a lot of little animals must die. It doesn't seem
exactly right. They lived their little animal lives. A clean
towel is a good morning. Coffee with milk. Here are the
ideas: a thick smog of gone days. Please. Lying on a hill
without bitterness. Some free sugar in a bowl. A secret
pity for the crows. Our pretty walk before dark. To cloud.
To be clouded. To dissipate. Yesterday I had to try harder
to appreciate everything. It wasn't seeming exactly right.
I had to really want to stay.

LUCKY POEM

Don't look for luck
It will come to you
— fortune cookie

If this fortune is found
scrounging under cushions
you've embarrassed yourself.
Sit down.

Sitting, imagine
luck is a bird, a starling
that shoos off the pecking flock.

Then stop. It's not right.
Luck must be a lovebird.

Start a trail of seeds for luck
on the windowsill that will lead
straight to your purring cupped palms.
If it seems luck will hop to you,
call this a prayer.

Don't pray too long.
Sing. Like a lovebird.
Practice luck's song to woo it.
Even moments later
when you find your whole arm
thrust under the couch,
keep singing.

HOW BIRDS WORK

A dream in the color of flight.
It's easy to forget birds
except it's day and they whistle.
I was dragging something with wings
still so very small and then
they woke me up!
Hummingbirds hanging there
don't really stop time.
And a flower, even a red
flower, isn't a memory.
Birds! Am I being unfaithful to time?
Who with a ribbon tied to its leg
still won't let me catch up.
I must leave my body to get there, leave now.
Come back with a twig on fire.
Where they pecked my breadcrumb trail.
Leather glove and blindfold, all birds be mine!
Calling, calling. Don't stay gone.
Even on a small and isolated island
no scientist can keep an accurate count
of the native thrushes. If you do catch one
and cut it open, you still
won't understand it any better.
Birds consist largely of air,
                              pockets in the bone.
Humans consist largely of memory.
                              Buoyed to now when we long
for the birds. We weep for the birds
busy remembering and downing their nests.
Busy forgetting their safety for roadkill.
How do I circle this nothing
and grow hungry for? A bird would not.

New species making homes in the wrong climate.
Teach them a word. Hello. Home.
How dainty they seem and their beaks pull meat.
Of the sky again or singing and hidden.
Who was promised wings. We
will be birds in sleep
and in forever sleep which we remember
under memory. No hands. Birds
when their little bodies
probably won't stay now.
A poor clavicle fused for wishing.
To be put just here. Now just here.
Then a bird pops out of a clock.

PEACE

*

Treat it like it should come with shoulder straps:
a backpack always forgotten on the bus seat.
Three days a week
at the Transit Council Lost and Found,
rummaging through a rumpled cardboard box.
It waits, wedged
between the cashless
wallets and single mittens.
There.
No one has taken it.

*

One afternoon, her jaw and tongue swelled
up like plums and she had to rest

five days. Neighbors came to help
with the children and the dishes.

Her husband came home early
from work. It had been years

since anyone had seen a look
of peace on her face

like the one with which she met
their understanding gazes.

*

It did circle us grown-ups
like ponies roped to a turnstile
and we are so stolid, yes, doing our best.

All the riding children feel too silly for their caramel apples
as they bob, wrinkling their noses at the smell.

They remember a polite thank you, hating us for being
greasy where our iron joints twist and not

just brimming with sugar cubes and soft.
It's a gyp.

*

There is honking
during rush hour.
The tails of a woman's
overcoat flap against
her calves as she bends
to her bags on the sidewalk.

A suddenly
present
man at his wheel misses
an entire green light
waiting for the possibility
of her knees.

*

The birds keep cracking
their heads on my windowpane—
every Spring it's close.

*

It gets in. It's silent
and so light you suspect

something has been stolen
from you. Like sleep,

enough sleep, underneath
a blanket that was tucked tight

for you: for you who never
asked.

 **Upon Arrival**

In order to arrive at what you are not,
  You must go through the way in which you are not.
And what you do not know is the only thing you know...

– T.S. Eliot
from "East Coker"

COMMON PRAYER

The kitchen is supposed to be Heaven.
The hot kitchen of gas burners
and boiling pots where the oven
is never turned off.
The chef is supposed to be God.
The thirsty chef sweating
while editing a dead ladybug
out of your greens.
The dining room is
a different world entirely with light
music and central air. The linens
seem too nice so you finger
your wallet. You are
supposed to be you: seated
at a table placing your order.
The Chef juliennes carrots beautifully
while picturing your stingy fingers on
your wallet. While you await your bisque,
you picture the chef, but he does not
have a pencil-neat mustachio
or crisp white frock.
This bistro is always crowded
and almost everyone gets just what
they asked for every time. Order
the same damn thing every day for
all the Chef cares. The Tired Chef,
the Only Chef, drinking an entire
pitcher of water and pulling
his special hat down from
a high shelf like a cloud from the sky.
He wipes his wet neck with a napkin
and appears briefly in the window

of the kitchen's double doors to
receive your compliments: your
compliments to the Chef, which
will never be enough.

YOUR TRAINWRECK HEART

is perfect. A trainwreck
that for eternity never
happens is perfect because
the brakes fail and fail and
still it smokes down
tracks that run through
a small town in me.
The tracks stop at the platform.
Upon arrival, your trainwreck was.
Days it's gone, it is. A permanent
finale. I say the name
of it. A contagion. Every day
I say the perfect runaway name
of the engine of it
and in some way that makes it so
the perfect engine idles
in my heart and my heart
is a perfect station.
What a mystery.
Your trainwreck heart accelerates
beyond the horizon so I don't
imagine the tracks ending.
I don't have to imagine
any perfect ending, in
which I don't believe.

PASSENGER VILLANELLE

Someone infused my eyelashes with lead.
My heavy eyelashes chew the horizon.
The horizon conjures a skyline.

The skyline is missing teeth.
Accuse the low muzzle of cloud:
they are the infusers of lead.

The windshield sings, they call it "rhinestone."
You sing while driving toward
the skyline the proud horizon presents.

Are we almost to Douglas? Chicago? Are we
almost home?   Some songs
in my eyes (something heavy is closing)

are pretty. Shut them tight. Songs
until now I didn't know you would sing.
The singular horizon and its sole skyline become

one thing. Only if I pretend to sleep will you sing.
We must live here. Between sleep
                    and your hand on my thigh.
Eyelashes floating the lead clouds will leave
a skyline behind us. Oh, the lonesome, lonesome horizon.

ST. PAUL PSALM

Unless right
        on the banks
                I still can't tell

west in this town.
        High hill, the cathedral
                where a spigot dispenses

holy water. And lower,
        and via paddleboat,
                our only source

delivers our sadnesses
        to the fishes.
                The burdened fishes

growing third eyes for us
        all the way to Mardis Gras.
                After a starting point:

everything.
        The names of streets
                in this town change

in the rain.
        On National
        Backwater Day,

our river
        does not reverse.
                It sings.

MERCURY WAITS TABLES
AT THE MACROCOSM CAFE

Yes, It's true. I kiss everyone. Except
certain men and women whose faces
sour at luncheon plates which

fail to meet their expectations.
Messenger between gods, I have a message:
                    The Kitchen Does Not Love You.

Stunned, you ask: if the kitchen will not
love us, then how
shall we be loved? By whom?
You ask: does the kitchen love

you? No, no. See how happily I don't expect
the kitchen's love.
                    : won't the kitchen love
                      a stood-up customer

whose table is haloed with absence:
prolonged hour of a refreshed
water glass and no dinner companion?

Not even the hungry shall earn the kitchen's love.

But now you think I want to kiss you. Or take
something from you. That isn't

what matters. The kitchen loves the kitchen
and through its rapture of self-love trickles
bounty down upon us.

Meanwhile, in a restaurant nice as this,
kissing is *de rigueur*. Forever
someone's birthday, promotion, lucky date...

O your parched lips await
your gleaming fork and spoon. See
the far away water pitcher?

I'll bring it for you.

LAMPPOST ELEGY

Lampposts are
so symbolic they are
nearly
impossible.
The dark
night between
the lampposts is,
and that we find
our way to the lamplight
by feel is
implied.
Anyone
standing below a lamppost
becomes illuminated,
becomes destined
to fail. But let's
still kiss once
within the lamppost halo.
Come morning,
we'll lean
disaffectedly
against the lampposts—
their weak light
looking extra
ancient in the bright sunlight—
while dandelions bloom
beneath, between
the millions
of visible cracks.

HISTORY, A ROUND

Our stories do
appear to constellate
like the little crows
that grow fat
as black snowflakes which
we desire to catch on our tongues.
When we are happy
we pretend to be rich
pitching dimes
from our hotel window. When
we are happy we believe
memory to be a kind of sheet
music we could
refer back to for any
exact tune, even
in our well-scrubbed sleep.
And how the Beauty of It All repeating
causes me to weep
between
rumpled blank sheets,
the millefleur pattern
of girlish tears for the precious
stories that constellate like crows
that grow cindery
as snowflakes we desire to catch
on our tongues when
we are happy

HERE ON SOMNAMBULIST AVENUE

the dogs dream leashed.
It's tough for lovers
to promenade, her arm
draped across his chest:
danger of ending, of endlessness;
one hates to be the first to wake.
Meanwhile, nothing at night
is green, stripped to the mechanics
of itself and no one paying attention.
Down the street, the windows of
buildings go dark, dark,

insomniac bulb,

dark, dark, dark, and etc.
A battalion of stars
doesn't matter.
One constellation loosens, visits
another, spilling borrowed salt.
Thusly does the universe expand
while the shut eyelids of babies flit
and the lips of mothers part softly
in gentle snores while pushing
carriages out into the street.

The last bulb goes out.

Someone sleepless prays:
Let whomever can recall
in dream the greenness
of one single blade of grass
by sunlight remain a believer
in green. Amen.

Moments later, the bulb is relit.

Who is that one forever
surprised come morning?

THE NEW SEMATOLOGY

A woman who's recently been talking too much finds
her heart's been reduced to a series of news articles.
She becomes quiet. Not as before, but as if she had
just broken a favored bowl. The man next to her
lays his head on her breasts and hears, far
out at sea, a metronome. He tells her this
and she pictures it. She pictures the pages
of the daily paper lining the ocean floor,
the headlines bleeding away while
the pulse of any song she might desire
floats somewhere close enough to listen
for, keeping perfect time. Perfect time. Perfect time.

OTHER WAYS TO SAY HEART

~ Private Jukebox

~ Conductor of Dumb Waiters

~ *To Kingdom the Human*

~ Loft

~ Body's Epigram

~ One Shoe in the Road

~ The Real
  Midwest of the Person

~ *Cause of Yawning*

~ Vehicle *Driven / By Internal
  Dogs*

~ Answering Machine

~ Emporium of One Way Streets

~ Occupied Land

~ Little Pet Who Will Not Always Eat From My Palm

~ One Hundred Sparrows Perch In a Diseased Elm

~ Condignity's Railroad

~ *Sound Like*
  a Pouch of Marbles Dropped
  Down Wood Steps

~ Canopy Covering a Lost House Key

~ Keeper
  of the Ceaselessly

~ Most
  Beautiful Mule

~ Open Palm

~ *A Book of Matches*
  Goes Off in her Shirt

DID I GLOW?

Suddenly, I felt bad
glowing: like a question mark.

Like I got someone's light-up
present by mistake. Anybody

missing a light up present? I
might have it here. I will

wrap it up for your birthday.
But let me just state that

though without it I will grow
homesick (like a question mark)

I don't know how this glowing
started. For all I know

it was here first.
By way of apology, I will

have to try to already
stop glowing. This isn't

your light-up present, is it?
Doesn't anybody like their own?

Once I did. I loved
everyone's glowing.

PIANO SOLO

– i.m. Bobby Peterson

On the tables of the club romantic
flames flicker flick, certainly
a kind of clock. A new guy on piano
tonight. Let's be a great audience.
Fingers are to keyboard as droplets
to river as eyes are to blue. See
keys. See also *contributary*. See with
your ears a brittle film from inside
the piano works of a piano player gone
missing. Already off in the wherever
writing original lost songs. (Fingertips
beyond us, a record.) Riff off
the weight of bodies going up and back
down. A staircase we know by heart.

ANEMOSCOPE

I heard the sky
        growing in the night:

            the wind was
                some giant breaths

                        from the West: Woosh! A dark
                            balloon being stretched.

                        I never slept. Today,
                I'm looking out a dollhouse window

            at a swollen sun, goliath clouds looming
    over toy cars on our fresh little streets, perfectly

    arranged. Tiny ants eat sleep-sap

off peony buds in my neighbor's garden.
Ridiculous sizes? Whatever blooms.

R.S.V.P.

I do   not mean   to squander   not knowing
by asking   I'm asking   a question

not as if I personally put the *quest* in question
as a smaller event   the size of an envelope

one question   wants something placed within it
something lovely   somewhat smaller than

not like a pin   for a rare butterfly
              or   *to prick thy finger and sign*

something neatly folded   might have
a little present hiding in itself (?)   No one asks

to get a present   ask to   please
never get a present   ask

to continue
the act   of opening

UPON ARRIVAL #37

I have lived in hotels
for years. I want for a parakeet.

I want for a philodendron
like back when. They say

you can't kill that plant, but
you can kill that plant.

You there, if suddenly
reminded of the words

to a song you never sing,
please sing it. Sing

right now. How I desire one day
to stand before a stove and, listening, ruin

your dinner. Though the preparations
were so elaborate. Though it was

going to be beautiful.

OPENING REMARKS

The correct packaging of my latest dirge
has come to a standstill.

Let us dance to the tune of a dead stop.
Let us begin the "Rather Be" Waltz.

It goes

Wearing a corsage while lambasting safeguards...

And later continues

robbing the unseemly junctions of power...

That's the song I love!
Who titled me Distributor of Dirges?
Did I consent?

I _____ the world. With all my garbled _____.
   verb   noun

Therefore I quit I quit
I quit my job!

The dirges piling off the conveyor belt
are someone else's responsibility!

I shall glide on, cotillion to prom,
with vigor, with commiseration

deviating attractively back

into the drama the drama the drama of the human spirit.

THE WORD STRING CAN'T BLISTER
YOUR HANDS

Someone says they've got a surprise
for you at the end of a string:

the etymology of your favorite thing's word.
With interest you follow the string around bedroom

corners, through dime-stores, and across ocean
floors until you find yourself

in an English pasture, staring at the end:
a little bow tied to the exo-skeleton

of a five hundred pound butterfly.
There is a note coiled in its proboscis like a good

dog with your slippers. Translated by the first
able stranger, the note

is said to read: *The wings
are perfectly preserved*

and somewhere in Iceland. You wonder
at how old you've become and who else

is not to be trusted
with language.

Paula Cisewski's poems have appeared in *Hunger Mountain*, *Black Warrior Review*, *Crazyhorse*, *Spinning Jenny*, *Forklift OH*, *Swerve*, and *Conduit*, among other magazines. She was born in Bemidji, MN, which is the first city on the Mississippi River and where the actual site of the birth of Paul Bunyan is marked by giant statues of both Paul and his blue ox, Babe, standing in front of a lakeshore carnival. A later generation of an immigrant family, Paula only learned to cook and curse in Polish. She received her B.A. from the College of St. Catherine in St. Paul, MN, and her M.F.A. from Vermont College. She and her son live in Northeast Minneapolis.

In the poem *Other Ways to say Heart*, italicized lines are borrowed lines from poems by Sarah Fox, Gabriella Klein, Kelly Everding, Brian Engel, and C.D. Wright.

The italicized line in *Having To Do With The Manner In Which We Transport Night* is John Ashbery's.